# One Second...

Beejal Mehta

BookLeaf Publishing

Presentation by *BookLeaf Publishing*

Web: www.bookleafpub.com

E-mail: info@bookleafpub.com

ISBN: 978-93-95755-91-7

First edition 2022

# DEDICATION

Would like to dedicate this book to my family
and friends, my parents and grandparents
especially...who were all there for me when I
needed it most!

# ACKNOWLEDGEMENT

I would especially like to thank Alan Hewitt, Carole Pound, Cressida Laywood, Basia Grybowska, Sharon Engel Baker, Jerry Johnson, Jasvinder Khosa, Kate Swinburn, Julie Hickin and not forgetting Nadia, Jane and Eva, and of course Kalpesh...thank you!

# PREFACE

This is a short poem by one of the strongest, most courageous women who lived throughout history (and she reminds me of my mum…!)

Still I Rise
– by Maya Angelou

You may write me down in history, with your bitter, twisted lies,
You may trod me in the very dirt, but still, like dust, I'll rise.

Does my sassiness upset you? Why are you beset with gloom?
'Cause I walk like I've got oil wells, Pumping in my living room.

Just like moons and like suns, With certainty of tides,
Just like hopes springing high, Still I'll rise.

Did you want to see me broken? Bowed head and lowered eyes?
Shoulders falling down like teardrops.
Weakened by my soulful cries.

Does my hautiness offend you? Don't you take it
awful hard
"Cause I laugh like I've got gold mines, Diggin'
in my own back yard.

You may shoot me with your words, You may
cut me with your eyes,
You may kill me with your hatefulness, But still,
like air, I'll rise.

Does my sexiness upset you? Does it come as a
surprise,
That I dance like I've got diamonds, At the
meeting of my thighs?

Out of the huts of history's shame, I rise
Up from a past that's rooted in pain, I rise
I'm a black ocean, leaping and wide,
Welling and swelling I bear in the tide.
Leaving behind nights of terror and fear, I rise

Into a daybreak that's wondrously clear, I rise
Bringing the gifts that my ancestors gave,
I am the dream and the hope of the slave.
I rise
I rise
I rise

# One second...

I was walking with my mum and dad,
Along the long and winding road,
When suddenly my left arm was hurting,
I thought I was about to implode.

I looked at my mum,
Then over to my dad,
I felt all funny inside.
My brain was aching,
My face was drooping,
However, it was only on one side.

My mouth couldn't speak,
Not one single word,
My arm went floppy as well.
My hands and my feet,
Surely couldn't meet,
I felt woozy, hazy, not well.

I collapsed, do tell,
Face down on the floor,
Faintly, I could hear the call.
My dad had his phone,
My mum wrapped me up,
And immediately, I felt small.

Like a baby, I was,
So helpless I felt,
Rapidly, I was in a dream.
Fairies and unicorns,
And clouds and rainbows,
Anything, to take me away from this theme.

Doctors and nurses,
And ambulance too,
All tried to wake and revive me.
They did the FAST test,
And so much more,
I had damage to my brain, inside me.

Then the therapists came,
To help me recover,
They were nice, jolly, and fun.
They had all types of gadgets,
Electric devices, mirrors and games,
The 'Little Red Riding Hood' book, my number
one.

I said my first word,
I made a small joke,
My friends, they laughed with glee.
They said, 'your back',
I said 'I'm getting there',
I kept on thinking, will I ever be free?

I asked 'how is school?'
I asked 'how is grandma?'
'I want to play baseball and dance!'
My voice was getting stronger,
My face was no longer drooping,
My arm and leg, now they needed a chance.

Wii tennis I played,
My balance was restored,
The mirror trick was entrancing.
I stepped outside,
Very anxious at first,
My neighbours and people were glancing.

I had a stick initially,
Very awkward and fussy,
Luckily mum was there to support me.
We went to the shops,
Cinema, bowling alley and café,
Felt I needed everyone to escort me.

Then the day came,
I finally went abroad,
I'd been wishing, wanting it for so long.
I still missed my friends,
My recovery wasn't over,
I didn't feel that I belonged.

Exams, university and my life,

Had to be put on hold,
Special needs school – really?
Not as a pupil, to volunteer,
I was so bored, thought might as well,
Then I met a fellow called 'Billy'.

My first friend, I thought,
After all of this havoc,
We were, near enough, alike,
He was low spectrum autistic,
Showed me some hints and tips,
When my parents surely did strike.

Friends are important,
No matter what you have,
They make light of mundane tasks,
We aided the other kids,
Finally, I could see light,
I was able to take away my mask.

A year or so went by,
I kept on improving,
Next I joined a charity.
More friends, more like me,
'Where've you been all our lives',
I smirked, I grinned, I was a rarity.

You see,
I was young, handsome, enigmatic,
And had a sense of humour,
Stroke, aphasia, multiple disabilities.
They weren't really a part of me,
Was I a commodity, service or a consumer?

Accessibility and limited function,
I certainly had to deal with that,
But I had,
Understanding, compassion, empathy,
I was ahead of the game.
Now that is a definite fact.

I became the head of finance,
Within the charity I started off with,
My story is one of success.
And sure we had our work banter,
Christmas and office parties too,
But there is still so much need to progress.

Disability rights,
Poverty,
Suicide.
Equality,
Discrimination,
One day, I hope, unified.

My very true friends,
Knew what I was like,
If they didn't,
They would soon learn.
With some manoeuvres, here and there,
Adaptation is key, without much concern.

Billy became part of my life,
He knew what it was like to be different,
I introduced him to my friends.
They could see why I liked him so much,
With him by my side,
Felt on top of the world, ascends, and ascends…

The next thing was a girl,
I'll finish the poem here,
Do not want to give away too much.
In hindsight, there were some hilarious times,
In the end I met my future wife.
Stroke affects everything, seeing, speaking and
touch.

But if you have,
A positive outlook on life,
Then it's not as hard as people make out.
Stroke is a biographical disruption, sure,
And disability really takes the biscuit,
But it's the people you surround yourself with,
you could never live without.

# Aphasia

Dyscalculia, apraxia, dysphasia, aphasia,
They didn't know what I had at first,
They thought it might have been epilepsy,
Or MS or just a plain and simple heart attack,
And I was talking funny because I was drunk.

Drunk, drunk…I had that quite a lot,
'Are you quite drunk? Tipsy? Hammered?'
You see, my speech was 'slurred' initially,
And some people didn't understand that,
Or they just didn't care.

Slurred and I would often 'miss words out'
I told someone once, 'I know your hair is black,
But I can't remember the word, 'black',
So I will say all the words linking around it,
'Dark', 'Charcoal', 'not light', 'dark brown'
etc…

Topsy turvy, back to front, inside out,
'It's all semantics' I would say,
Not really knowing at the time what that word
meant,
Broca's or Wernicke's,
What's the difference? I asked.

Broca's aphasia is expressive aphasia,
The non-fluent type,
I think having Wernicke's aphasia is often
worse,
I would write down in my notebook initially,
'Fairy tinker Christmas lights'

Meaning that 'I wanted a drink, that I was
thirsty…'
It was nonsense, absolute nonsense,
As my head was in a haze,
Felt like I wanted to communicate,
So I would communicate anything,

Wide variety of people at the support group,
Some could not speak, at all, but could express,
Themselves in other ways,
Some had other disabilities affecting the
Eyes, the arms, the feet, the mouth.

They were welcoming, all different creeds,
Had one thing in common though,
We were all rehabilitating and recovering,
So we built up a bond,
It seemed ever lasting,
They were there when I needed it.

# Mind

I did not wonder where I was,
I could not see my mother's startled, sorrowful
face,
I was not scared of what had become of me,
I did not try to speak,
I did not try to move my hand, arm, and
shoulder,
I did not try to walk,
I had not lost my balance,
I was not tired,
I did not wake up and sleep late,
I was not so frustratingly bored with doing the
same things,
I did not have to put my life on hold,
I did not shed a tear,
I did not weep,
I did not have to alter my career,
I did not feel like I was losing my identity,
I did not feel demotivated at times,
I did not feel as though all my efforts had gotten
me nowhere,
My heart was not racing,
I did not feel emotional,
I did not feel anxious,
I was not depressed.

I did find support at a charity,
I did make true friends at this support group,
They did teach me so much,
They were there for me when I was questioning everything,
I did adapt my career path,
I did find motivation,
My body was getting stronger,
I did find things which I would have done without otherwise,
I found that I could speak more fluently,
I did find ways of adapting,
People did support me on things that I couldn't do,
I did find creativity in other ways,
I did find solace in gardening, and music, and art,
I did get involved,
I did run a race,
I did raise lots of money,
I did keep a positive mindset,
I did find peace.
I did find love.

# She has a disability...

She has a disability,
It's on her hands,
I don't think it's on her legs?
She couldn't speak,
Did she tell you that?
She is nice otherwise,
Oh gosh, she's not even married yet,
Will she ever get married?
Are her parent's ok?
How is her family coping?
She can't drive anymore,
Did she tell you that?
How is her work?
She can't be a doctor anymore,
What will she do for money,
How is her physio going?
Does she speak alright right now?
She speaks alright,
We should do something for her?
Don't want to step on anybody's toes though,
She loved to paint,
Can she still do that?
She must be able to,
Not as well though,
She can't cook anymore,

Did she tell you that?
Oh no, she loved to bake,
She used to love swimming,
Can she still do that?
Can she go out?
Can she go on holiday?
Can she speak to an assortment of people, the
way she used to?
Only time will tell…

# Struck down...

He was working a 9-5 job,
She was unemployed.

He had a wife and 3 little girls to support,
She was single, living the bachelorette life.

He had a house, a car, with bills to pay,
She was renting a flat, and living in the city.

Then suddenly, he was struck down,
Then suddenly, she was struck down.

His wife helped him up, his kids were
frightened,
Luckily, she was able to call the ambulance.

The ambulance came, they checked his vitals,
She did the FAST test, she was slowly drooping.

What have you had, his daughter asked in the
ambulance?
She had had a stroke…

His bed was next to another person,
She wanted to be alone.

The next morning, the sun shone through his
eyes,
Her very best friends came to visit her.

He awoke, and could utter some words,
She could now talk, semi-fluently.

His wife was weeping, he smiled as he saw his
children,
Her friends tried to make jokes and keep her
positive.

His daughter had brought him a balloon,
Her friends had brought trashy magazines with
pictures,

The nurse had been so helpful to him,
Over the next couple of days, the doctor came to
see her.

You've had a TIA she said,
You gave us quite a fright he said but with
plenty of rehab you should make it through.

He looked at her for the very first time,
She glanced at him and for the very first time,
shed a quiet tear.

# Self

Self.

Self esteem,
Self esteem,
Self esteem,
Self esteem,
Self esteem,
Self esteem,
Self esteem,

Self confidence,
Self confidence,
Self confidence,
Self confidence,
Self confidence,
Self confidence,

Self determination,
Self determination,
Self determination,
Self determination,
Self determination,,

Self assurance,
Self assurance,

Self assurance,
Self assurance,

Self reliance,
Self reliance,
Self reliance,

Self possession,
Self possession,

Self…

# There is always light...

Constant Struggle,
Will I ever be Happy again?
I feel so Alone,
Is time really a Healer?
Pit of Darkness,
Can't seem to find any Escape?
Always going through Ups and Downs,
Will I always be this Insecure?
I am Isolated, Alone and Unhappy,
Will this Torture never end?
I am down at my Lowest Point
Am I really Mentally Unstable?
Feels like an Endless tunnel,
Do I have to keep Burrowing through?
Like I'm Submerged under water,
Can't find air to Breathe?
I need some Space,
Am I Overcrowding you?
Constantly Tired, Lethargic,
Why does everything Irritate me?
Don't seem to have any Energy,
Is it really this Severe?
Severe Emotional pain,
Is that the Anxiety talking?
I feel Broken inside,

Will I ever be Okay again?
In Mourning, Grief-stricken,
I don't know what to do with my Life?
Is this what they talk about when they describe
the Dark days…
Will I ever Love life?

It will pass,
You will find a way,
Give it time,
Be kind,
Be caring,
Be compassionate,
There is always light…

# Your look may have changed...

Your appearance may have changed,
Whether you're male
or female too.
Your face may feel a bit droopy,
Arms and legs, flailing about,
And your skin may feel a bit odd at first too.

Rather than walking upright,
You may have to sit in a wheelchair,
Or with crutches or a stick.
Rather than eating with both hands,
You may have to use adaptations,
Like a fork, with a knife and a wick.

Driving hmmm – perhaps with an adapted car,
You may feel a bit wobbly initially,
And your shoes shouldn't have laces.
Learn to use the bus, tram and train,
I say wobbly as your balance may be affected,
And rucksack – in certain places.

Your arm may have arthritis,
After a long while,
Why its good to have some aid.
Watch, bracelet, and bangles,
May need to switch hands,
Why its good to have some aid.

Your nails may need to be polished,
Your eyebrows may need to be done,
That's the beauty of having mums, sisters and
friends,
They can help you look your brightest,
So you can face the world with armour,
weaponry,
Thus you don't have to descend…

Overall, having a stroke isn't so bad,
Disability part does suck,
Slowly, you will find strength,
You never knew you had,
Friends – you may have to rely on a lot,
But the friends who stuck by you,
Are family, through and through,
And they will be there for you no matter what…

# Left brain Vs. Right brain

Left brain Vs. Right brain,
Ischaemic Vs. Haemorrhagic,
Broca's Vs. Wernicke's,
FAST Vs. Silent stroke,
TIA Vs. mini stroke,
Dreams Vs. hallucinations,
Rehabilitation Vs. recovery,
Adult Vs. child,
Brain Vs. rest of body,
Disability Vs. death,
Walking Vs. running,
One Vs. both eyes,
Tumours Vs. aneurysms,
Vascular dementia Vs. series of strokes,
Age related Vs. infancy,
Cold Vs. hot,
MRI Vs. CT,
Heart Vs. Blood,
Blood clot Vs. Bleeding,
Surgery Vs. Treatment,
Thrombolysis Vs. Clot buster,
Depression Vs. Anxiety,
Psychological Vs. Cognitive,
Movement Vs. Communication,

Swallowing Vs. Visual,
Sex Vs. Driving,
Bladder Vs. Bowel,
High blood pressure Vs. high cholesterol,
Diet Vs. Exercise,
Smoking Vs. Alcohol,
Analytical Vs. Creative,
Left brain Vs. Right brain.

# Everchanging chasm

Life is like an ever-changing chasm,
Constantly rocking, twisting, spinning,
Like a rollercoaster.
Was constantly divided between
the rich and the poor,
the old and the young,
the black and the white,
(and the yellow and brown in between).
We had up and downs,
Passionate embraces and tears straight after,
Hormones, endorphins after strenuous exercise,
Feats of confidence, of empowerment,
Followed by new founded ways of creativity.
Disability doesn't equal ability,
For certain situations - Or does it?
We can all ask for help – if we do,
Aren't we changing human thought?
Like female, black and ethnic minorities, lgbtq+.
Aren't I an artistic expression of the
imagination,
Constant looking and longing,
Tattoos, graffiti, modern dance and theatre.
Aren't they standing up to 'The Man'.
I thought then,
That's ok,

Life is made up of a variety of life.
We should give to the poor,
and rejoice with the rich.
Celebrate the colour of life!

# And then the pandemic hit...

There once was a pandemic,
Covid 19 it was called,
It came from Italy and China,
Both men and women had to stay locked up,
indoors.

Coronavirus, furlough and lockdown,
Soon became synonymous with our country,
It spread all across the world it seemed,
Ages, races, genders, no discrimination, it knew
no boundaries.

Or so we thought…

Boris, Sunak, Starmer, Whitty, Priti,
Sturgeon, Trump, Biden, and even Evans got
involved!
Soon everyone became glued to the television
nightly,
To see what the latest update was.

Went from 1st dose, to 2nd dose to 3rd,
Like a whirlwind, spinning, like a rollercoaster,
No one really understood at first,
So many unanswerable questions,

Vaccinations, covid passes, NHS queues rose,
Unemployment increased,
Travel was restricted and then some,
Red, amber and green list,
Certified, authority, passenger locator form etc
Will it never end?

The research was too quick,
The timeline was too fast,
Rapidly became like an American government,
Kissing, philandering, and boozy parties,
But in the end, the most vulnerable suffered.

Is the graph the reporters showed on the news
really accurate?
Are the NHS queues for vulnerable patients that
high?
Can kids go back to school yet?
Will the education system have to change as
well?
Everyone is kinder, but is that enough?
Can no one stand up for the little guy anymore?

I don't understand…
I don't understand…
I don't understand…
Perhaps we never will….

# Damn politics

Always keeping a watchful eye,
Be it Disability rights,
Or the Equality or Discrimination Act,
Or the Data Protection Act,
All comes down to human rights.
We must fight for them,
It's our civic duty,
We must strive,
We must protest,
Those before us, look how far they've come,
We now have disabled freedom passes,
We now have help with our living expenses,
We can now go to the cinema,
We have disability specific shops,
And items to purchase,
We have charities,
We have the Paralympics,
And entertainment all about disability,
Words like accessibility,
Now mean something!
Individuals who can't quite manoeuvre,
That's ok – as we have the new age of DIGITAL
Individuals can virtually speak to each,
And that's taken as ok!
Having mental health/complex issues,

That's ok too,
There's still more to be done,
So much more,
To make sure that the smaller people,
Do not get trodden on by the almighty fat cats.
It has always been the time for 'Ability'
Yes in this country,
But what about the next?
…
Always keeping a watchful eye,
Office politics,
Damn politics!

# Daydream...

If only I could win the lottery,
Then I would by a big house,
And several fancy cars,
And several large businesses,
I would ride horses,
And swim in swimming pools,
Buy designer bags and shoes,
And take my friend and family on expensive
holidays,
I could go on 'pimp my ride',
Or Grand Designs,
Would buy a yacht,
And go on a year long voyage,
Discovering the foreign lands.
Would take helicopter lessons,
And deep sea diving too,
And only the best of healthcare
For me and my loved ones.
I would buy apartments in 7 continents,
And would have a swiss bank account,
As that is all the rage!
I would open a foundation,
To give to the poor and needy,
Would buy several bars,
And would hold the most exquisite events,

I would own a basketball team,
And cricket too,
I would train in the Olympics,
And become a public speaker too,
I would ride on the orient express,
I would open a stage, a theatre,
Or a studio,
Somewhere people could go to be themselves,
Dance, sing, or act,
I would run for governor,
Err actually…
Naah,

My daydream……
My wish…
Fingers crossed…
X

# Mind's eye

Mind's eye is a wonderful thing,
Can help you see things you never thought
possible,
Mind's eye was so vivid,
So clear,
So crisp,
I could almost taste it,
It was so graphic,
So colourful,
So unique.
Was like thinking in radio terms,
Imagination is so picturesque,
Relax,
Gently enter into a deep sleep,
Deep slumber,
And you can visualise it,
It was a leg kicking a football,
But it was inside out,
Upside down,
Perception,
Visualisation,
Imagination,
Conception,
Recollection,
Suggestion perhaps?

…and very sharply and abruptly awake!

One, two,
Three, four,
Look over to your left,
And over to your right,
And now up,
And down,
Mhmph…
One side of your vision has been affected,

Ahhh…

# Trick not to twist

Venturing outside can be tricky,
Especially initially,
Especially if you don't know if your legs will
work,
Due to the sheer burden of going outside,
Like you always did before,
You're carer will push you to do so many things
that you're not used to anymore,
Like venturing outside,
Or tying up your shoes,
Or making a cup of tea,
Such simple things,
Taken for granted,
Trick is to take a deep breath and focus,
Focus on what you're doing,
Forget everything else around you for a moment,
Just focus,
Do not turn,
Do not twist,
Just breath…
…and focus…
And you will get there,
At your own pace,
And your loved ones will be there to support
you…

Just breath and focus…
Breath and focus…
And before you know it,
You can do it at the click of a button…

# Who's who of devices??

What is that?
My young niece asked…
What do you think it is?
It looks like a playset for the beach…?!
That looks funny…
This one sticks!...It's smooth, but sticks…!
This one looks like a huge basketball?!
You can try your walking stick out as a laser…
Zooommm…zooommm,
All your cutleries made out of plastic?!...that's a
bit odd,
but really fab… you can take them out on
picnics!
Where is the creepy, robotic one?
That is my favourite one of all…
That's a specialist hand device,
Kind of like …,
Or are you too young for that?
Can you catch a ball with it…?
You can!
Where are your funny looking glasses?
Do you know what this is?
Can you see through it?
Each of these minute little rolls with sharp edges

Are very small prisms…
Ooohh…
Can you really see…like me?
Well my visual field, my vision on the outside, is
a little bit blurred,
but nothing that I can't get over,
but with the prism, yeh, I can see pretty well
Can you really walk…like me?
If it's a bright sunny day
And I have my trusted walking stick,
Then I can walk a few miles, I kid you not…
Hmmm…
Its ok, I'll walk with you
And so they did
Hand in hand
Hand in hand

# Support groups

If you join a charity,
There are various support groups you can join,
If you have a disorder, or an anomaly of some kind,
They can be a kind of therapy,
As everybody is going through it,
At all types of different levels, everybody!

You can firstly go with a friend,
A friend is good, if you're feeling a bit anxious at
first,
You're then 'let loose' into the wild,
The wild, as in individuals trying to recover (just like
you),
There might be volunteers, members and staff
members alike,
And they might ask to, one day, even be a volunteer
yourself.

You can join several groups,
Groups for what you're interested in,
Or what may help you to get back on your feet,
Get back on your feet you will, as there may be a
conversation group, or a physio group, or a wellbeing
group,
Or you might to have a natter at the coffee and cake
group,
They serve lots of teas and coffees at the drop-in
session as well.

There will be someone there to get you involved in something else,
Like an event of some kind, you could be involved in,
Or a research project, or a model, or a social media star,
Star, you could be pictured on a poster, or a booklet,
You even be on a TV ad, and speak at several conferences,
Both national and if you're lucky, international conferences.

You'll make friends and comrades along the way,
And along the way you may get to meet some influential people,
But the important thing is that you are involved,
You are involved and engaging with others,
You have a voice, no matter how small or large it is,
You can speak for people who don't have voices,

You are all going through this together,
Together you stand…

# Intimacy and disability

Having someone who has your back at all times,
Someone that you chose,
To be in your life,
To be in your world,
Through thick and thin,
When times get tough,
And sure enough they will,
You feel close enough to tell them anything,
Your hopes and fears,
Your dreams and sacrifices,
No belittling, no judging, just you…
They only have your best interests at heart,
If you can't tell them, that's ok…
With a look, a glance, tiniest gesture
They will know…
Close enough to feel, to touch, to sense their
presence,
Without even having to open your eyes,
It's an intoxicating human scent,
You can't help but be near them,
You feel safe, secure around them,
You have an instant connection,
May be from so long ago,
May be from the present moment,
Some may call it 'chemistry',

Some may say 'kismat',
Some may say 'lust'…
Soulmate,
Perhaps…
Surely it cannot be love??
Can one find intimacy in sex?
Perhaps…
Or friendship?
Perhaps…
Or a relationship of any kind…
Perhaps…
It is whatever you feel it is…

Physical or mental disability is perhaps the most
difficult hurdle to bypass in order to achieve
intimacy,
But once you do,
It takes your breath away…

# Diagnosis?

Cerebrovascular disease
Anatomy of the brain and spinal cord
Vascular neurologist
Consultant
Blood vessels in the frontal lobe
Frontal cortex
Ischemic
Haemorrhagic
Psychiatry
Therapist
TIA
Thrombectomy
Thrombolysis
Functional Electrical Stimulation (FES)
Mirror therapy
Neuroplasticity
Expressive Vs. Receptive aphasia
Health & wellbeing
Embolism
Facial weakness
History of vascular disease
Atherosclerosis
Cholesterol
Pins and needles
Smoking
Survivor
Diagnosis…
…Stroke

# With an essence of gratitude...

…with an essence of gratitude
Cheers, to all the doctors who saw me, helped
and continue to aid me from the world over,
Cheers to the therapists, who challenged me
when I thought I could not challenged,
Who made me see things, that if I hadn't had
this unfortunate incident, I wouldn't have seen,
Cheers to the nurses, who went running around
after the doctors, to make sure they made no
mistakes,
Cheers, to all my crazy family and friends, who
have been my routine throughout the rocky
times,
And cheers finally, to the little people,
to the security guards, the taxi drivers, the
restauranteurs,
and the customers of any place where I was
working, especially the difficult ones,
as they challenged me to keep going throughout
my career and then some…
Cheers to all these people,
and countless others, who made me a little bit
different, a little bit quirky,

made me have a little bit of a wild side, and
ultimately made me the person I am today,
Who wants to be 'normal' anyway,
I certainly don't,
To them I say thank you for giving me some
character…

# Funny thing about disability...

Funny thing about disability,
Makes you miss some chords on an instrument,
You can't quite recall what people are saying,
Words, sentences equal topsy, turvy and inside
out,
Where you see dreams others may see
hallucinations,
At times your sentences might miss a beat,
Your lyrics may overlook some notes,
Sometimes your brushwork may miss a stroke,
Your messages and texts may not make sense to
some,
Your visual field may be reduced,
Hemianopic…or anything else,
Not so crisp with less clarity,
Your art isn't quite the way you planned,
You may not be able travel or drive the way you
used to,
Hence, you have to adapt,
Have to have support,
Have to transform,
Have to be flexible,
Your mind and your body,
Needs time to rehabilitate or adapt,
You will certainly wobble,

and lose your balance,
Are your other senses heightened?
Some friends may be there for you,
And some you may think are not,
May be there in strange ways,
Like you've never expected,
Meanwhile you'll make new friends along the
way,
Without a doubt,
For all the weird and wonderful things,
There is hope,
There is laughter,
And it definitely gives you character,
You see strength where you didn't before,
As you are the definition of 'unique',
Have gone through awful things,
And come out smiling on the other side,
You are the real superheroes!

Funny thing about disability,
… and life in general…

* 9 7 8 9 3 9 5 7 5 5 9 1 7 *